Dear

Hope this is full of good ideas!!

Me xx 15/01/12.

You Talkin To Me?

You Talkin To Me?

Thoughts & Observations on Marketing & Promotions

Marc Apple

iUniverse, Inc.
New York Lincoln Shanghai

You Talkin To Me?
Thoughts & Observations on Marketing & Promotions

iUniverse, Inc.

For information address:
iUniverse, Inc.
2021 Pine Lake Road, Suite 100
Lincoln, NE 68512
www.iuniverse.com

ISBN: 0-595-32824-5

Printed in the United States of America

AUTHOR'S NOTE

While this book is a work of nonfiction, I have taken certain storytelling liberties to help move the events along, but it has been my intent to stay true to the stories as they took place.

In addition to those changes, I have made changes to protect the privacy of those mentioned. In no way, does this change the basis of the stories or the lessons to be taught.

"Once in a while you get shown the light
in the strangest of places
if you look at it right"

—Robert Hunter

ACKNOWLEDGEMENTS

The one and only NonaStar, my wife, best friend and editor. Need I say more? You are my perfect second set all rolled up into one. Thank you for letting my space be everywhere at once and never putting the brakes on all of my crazy ideas. 143.

To Mom, Dad, Robert and Barbra, thank you for never discouraging me. Without family and the support you give I would have never been able to do this. You have been with me when the chips were down and when the tide was high. Much love. Much respect. I know you've got my back.

Papa Sid, you showed me more in a handful of years than I could ever learn in a lifetime. From the opening note of a big band jump to how to make the best damn pickles around you stole the show and I am merely the opening act. Grammy, you hold my bawls and put me in place even if you are laughing with me while doing it. I'm glad I have you to call on my way home.

They're a band beyond description. Billy, Brent, Bruce, Bobby, Donna, Jerry, Keith, Mickey, Pig Pen and Phil. Thank you good ol' Grateful Dead. I've seen the music play the band and it will never be the same. RIP.

About A Boy. Almost Famous. Barkley. Beastie Boys. Black Flag. Buena Vista Social Club. Business 2.0. Calle Ocho. China Cat. Chocolate. Circle Jerks. Dawson's Creek. Del Fuegos. Etta James. Fast Company. Grant's All Spice. Japan. Jim Rome. Jimmy Scott. LA Dodgers. Lester's Diner. LL Cool J. Magnum PI. Melrose Place. Minor Threat. Mojitos. Momus. MTV. My Bodyguard. Nava. Nick Hornby. Peter McWilliams. Rider. Robbie Williams. Run DMC. Single malt scotch. Stan Call Neil. Sweetwater 420. Team Waffle House. The Doors. The Screaming Liberals. Usenet groups. Vic-Ar Court BBQ crew. Wired. Word up to my South Florida homies. Hollaback yo.

Starbucks Quad Venti Black and White Mocha. Amen.

"What's past is prologue."

—From Shakespeare's *The Tempest*

CONTENTS

"I wouldn't have turned out the way I was if I didn't have all those old-fashioned values to rebel against."

—Madonna

"Welcome to the jungle, we got fun and games…"

—Guns N Roses

INTRODUCTION

READ ME FIRST!

Welcome. There is only one rule for this book and that is, *You Talkin To Me? Thoughts & Observations on Marketing & Promotions* is not meant to be read from cover to cover in one sitting. In fact, I encourage you to not read the book in the order it has been laid out. This is your journey and you are free to pick and choose what you read and when. Flip the book open and read whatever page you land on. Scan the table of contents and see what suits your fancy. Ask the person next to you to guess a number between one and 125 and see what topic you've picked for today's reading. I wrote *You Talkin To Me? Thoughts & Observations on Marketing & Promotions* in hopes that you will take your time and come back often. Take what you need when the moment is there and put it aside when you are about to go on to something else.

I have always described marketing and promotions as one part of the action that makes you think you need something when you really don't. It's the best mind game out there and one that has been practiced for centuries. Take a moment and think about this, do you really need another brand of soda? Do you really need another detergent to clean your clothes or a new way to sweep up your kitchen floor? I'm not too sure you do.

Don't get me wrong I have practiced this ancient art for some time now and at the end of the day I love it. The act of fooling you into believing you need something, anything, is one I can't get enough of. I wouldn't have it any other way. Really. Of course there is more to marketing and promotions than fooling you. I was just being simple. As you read on you will see what I really mean by that.

Take a moment and think about this, where else are you given the opportunity to share with the world a story, an idea or an item but with marketing and promotions? Or maybe it's not something new at all but something that has been updated—or as they say in the business "new and improved." With marketing and promotions you are given the chance to expose and enhance the lives of others even if it's not life changing. And the reality is that most of the stuff out there isn't life changing. No matter how much you think it is, it really

"The funniest thing is when somebody says "Look I've no idea who you are but my friend said you are on a show and I just wanted to introduce myself" you know that they are lying! Those people can just get out of my way."

—Matthew Perry

isn't. Trust me on this one. Break it down and it really is just plain...are you ready for this? It really is, in one word, neat.

Don't worry, that confused look mixed with a smile on your face is fine. That's what I was looking for from you. And you didn't disappoint me. *Webster's Dictionary* defines the word neat as "*marked by tasteful simplicity*." Now does it make sense to you? It's ok if it doesn't. Read on and you will see that the neatness you bring to every situation you are in is what makes you, you. It is what makes marketing and promotions so unique because each of us brings our own perspective to it with hopes that others will share in what we have to say. With each promotion you are trying to make a connection to another human being. Sometimes we succeed and other times we fall flat on our faces but if we don't try we will never make contact. This is what makes marketing and promotions the best gig around.

You Talkin To Me? Thoughts & Observations on Marketing & Promotions is meant to provoke your thought process. This is your opportunity to talk back. Take time with each chapter. After you read it take a moment and think about what was said. Do you agree with it or have I got it all wrong?

Now go and grab that double shot of espresso, sit back, relax and get ready to explore my observations and thoughts on marketing and promotions.

Marc Apple
www.marcapple.com
Atlanta, Georgia–2004

"Great thoughts speak only to the thoughtful mind, but great actions speak to all mankind."

—Theodore Roosevelt

THOUGHTS

Right or wrong we all have thoughts on everything from the best show on TV to the worst car on the market. We each have our favorite band and movie that is number one in our collection. We believe what we believe based on our own experiences and what we have read or been told by others. These thoughts will dictate our actions.

One of the many functions of the brain is to make sure that you are right all the time. The brain doesn't know wrong. This is the reason why you will continue to make your case to others even when they are telling you you are wrong. We all do it. It's just the way it is, right or wrong.

You need to have the will power to open your mind to a new way of thinking. Step outside of your comfort zone and go against your first impulse of always being right. It might not work all the time but when you are willing to let your mind take in something new you will be surprised with the results.

Have fun!

"The power of accurate observation is commonly called cynicism by those who have not got it."

—George Bernard Shaw

OBSERVATIONS

Take a moment to sit back and observe and I bet you will learn something. Take a look and let the world in and what you once thought of as fodder soon can become the stuff that runs your life. Let the observation process take place and miracles happen.

Open your eyes and your mind will follow. By doing this you will give yourself that chance to experience all that is out there.

Open your eyes and let the world speak to you. Listen to what others are saying around you and what others say to you. Pay attention.

Say hello to that stranger you see every morning at the gym or on the bus on the way to work. Yes, I know it's scary but it won't hurt you, I promise. Go ahead and take that trip you always wanted even though it is only 50 miles away.

You just need to make a small effort to observe and the rewards will come at you at lighting speed. Open yourself up to the possibilities starting right now.

"To have ego means to believe in your own strength."

—Barbra Streisand

THE EGO HAS LANDED

I only do things one way.

That way is 110%.

For the life of me I can't understand doing anything less than that.

I either go all out or I don't go at all.

You are either in my scope or you are not.

You are part of the solution or part of the problem whether you like it or not.

The choice is yours.

Don't should on yourself.

Just be!

*"There's very little advice in men's maga-
zines,
because men think, I know what I'm doing.
Just show me somebody naked."*

—Jerry Seinfeld

WHAT'S WHAT

When I was fourteen years old I started my own national music/lifestyle fanzine. It was nothing fancy but it served its purpose which was one, an outlet for me to meet the bands and people that were driving my creative spirit and two, a way for me to kick start my writing career at such a young age.

The staff of *What's What* was made up of me, myself and I. It was a one-man show with the help of my father. It was he who drove me to the over 21 and up clubs and waited with me by the dumpsters in back alleys so I could try to score an interview with my new favorite band. I can't think of one time I wasn't successful landing an interview that I set out to get.

Because of my age I found that publicity departments at record companies really didn't take me seriously so I would always make sure I gave my best sob story to the artist directly and they just couldn't say no—call it beginner's luck, if you will.

The fanzine would consist of my interviews with the bands and pictures I had taken of them while they answered my questions. Keep in mind the PC had yet to reach the level it is at now, so I would cut and paste what I had typed up on a typewriter to sheets of paper and prepare them to be photocopied and stapled at my dad's office after hours or on the weekend.

The magazine continued for many years including into my late teen years when the drinking age was still twenty-one and I was not. But that never stopped me. There was only one real nightclub in town where the bands I was interested in talking to played. At least three nights a week I would find myself at The Cotton Club. At first, I would walk in confidently and tell the door girl that "I was on the list," which usually caused enough of a distraction that they would not ID me. As time went on I would just walk in, on the list or not. And then one day, a new person started working at the club and I bet you can guess what happened next. As I walked in my heart started to race and a slight fear came over me. I was about to be carded. I had always been nice and polite to the staff and that was about to pay off. Barry the manager came over and escorted me into the club without any hesitation. Turns out he was really surprised that I wasn't of age but that didn't stop him from giving me a lecture that included allowing me to come back anytime I wanted as long as I didn't drink. That was fine with me; I was there for the music first and foremost.

"A magazine is simply a device to induce people to read advertising."

—James Collins

The lesson here is quite clear, be nice to whomever you meet because you never know when it is going to come back and help you out.

"Rock 'n' roll is ridiculous. It's absurd. In the past U2 was trying to duck that. Now we're wrapping our arms around it and giving it a great big kiss."

—Bono of U2

BONO OPENS UP THE BACK DOOR

It's 1983 and the nearly sold out Sunrise Musical Theater is on its feet. Close to five thousand fans strong are cheering for the headline act to hit the stage. The band tonight is U2 who at the time are still relatively unknown in the United States but you wouldn't be able to guess that judging by the way the crowd was singing and screaming to every song they played.

At the time U2 were the biggest band in the underground alternative music scene and this was their first tour of some pretty big venues. Without a doubt you knew that this was going to be one of those last times you were going to see the band in this type of intimate setting. Soon everyone you knew would find out who they were and the specialness would be gone. And while that fact hung in the air, the band did not disappoint, from opening note to closing goodbye they gave it their all.

Now there's no need to go into detail about the history of U2. After the War Tour the band exploded like we knew it would. They eventually landed on the cover of every magazine and in the CD collection of your not so hip neighbor who lived down the street. There was a time when it seemed like you couldn't turn on the radio or TV without seeing or hearing about the Dublin Foursome. It drove me crazy.

And with this popularity came the shutting of doors. And I mean that literally. You see after that concert in 1983, a few of us stood by the backstage door waiting for the band to board their bus. At best, I was hoping to get my picture taken with The Edge and at the very least I would take an autograph. Hell, I would have even taken a handshake from their bus driver if it came down to it. Well, none of that took place instead what did take place was something very special.

Without any notice the security guard at the backstage door stepped aside and out came Bono. After a quick look around he invited the small group of us out of the dark and in to the backstage area. We sat and talked about tonight's concert, touring the U.S. and their music. All four of the band members were there and it was a blast I tell ya.

"Advertising and art are getting all mixed up.
I think some of the most exciting pieces of TV are the commercials."

—U2's The Edge

Shortly after that meeting a funny thing happened, U2 became so big I stopped liking them. Really, I just stopped, even with them being so cool to me that night. Looking back on it, I didn't buy another U2 record or see them live until 18 years later! I just didn't care anymore. And after that great Louisville concert I waited by the back door and was quickly asked to leave by some guy that resembled a large wall of pain. Ouch.

"Just play. Have fun. Enjoy the game."

—Michael Jordan

L.W.P.A.

L. Listen.

W. Wear.

P. Play.

A. Attend.

These are the four basic principals on how a consumer can interact with your marketing plans.

They will listen to what you have to say. You only have less than 10 seconds to capture their attention so you better make it quick and you better make sure it speaks volumes to them. With the ever shrinking attention span of most Americans, I would say that 10 seconds is really like 5 seconds with a bonus 5 if you've got them after the first 5 have passed. My advice is to be smart about what you say and obviously make it quick.

They will wear what you give them. They will wear what you tell them. They will wear what they see others wear. Watch what happens the next time you see someone giving away a free T-shirt. The people in the audience will go crazy for it. Why all the screaming for a $5 T-shirt? Because they have created a level of excitement for an item you can't just buy in any old Target store. Display you wearables in newspaper ads or have models wear them on the catwalk. With the right amount of publicity you could be the next Donna Karan. What makes her clothes so different from yours?

Consumers will play along with you and be happy to purchase what you have to sell. This is why in store sampling is so huge. Consumers like to know what they are getting into before they make a purchase. But once they do, you've got them in your back pocket. Give them a free sample. Give them a free tasting. Give them a piece of collateral material to take home. Let them play with you.

Consumers want to get out of the house. Give them something to attend. Given a reason they will come out and support you both with their presence

"Never play peekaboo with a child on a long plane trip. There's no end to the game."

—Rita Ruder

and wallet. From a football game at the stadium to a fashion show at the mall we all love to attend events. What are you attending today?

Exercise: For the next week keep a log of how you listen, wear, play and attend. I bet you will be surprised at how much you do.

"I wrote a song, but I can't read music
Every time I hear a new song on the radio
I think, "Hey, maybe I wrote that."

—Steven Wright

DO YOU KNOW WHO SINGS THAT SONG?

In high school, I was so punk rock. I had the mohawk, the combat boots, the band t-shirt and an attitude to match. I also knew a little more about the music than my peers. This made trivia my game of choice but it also forced the rest of the crew to find their own game.

We were all in love with these great bands that we heard on the radio. When I say on the radio, what I really mean is on the "Off the Beaten Path" radio program that aired Monday nights at midnight. This three-hour program was our only outlet to hear the type of bands that we enjoyed. And what did we care how tired we were on Tuesday morning; we only had school to go to.

My friend Larry found his game with an opportunity that played right into what we were all about, the music and being able to listen to it when we wanted to. Here's what Larry did. He got his mom to let him use her tax ID number and he started buying records directly from distributors. As the records came in, he would sell them to us at school for a modest profit. What a great idea!

Taking his mini business one step further he started contacting concert promoters about setting up shop in the lobby of their concerts. Within no time, Larry's record shop was off the ground and he was becoming quite popular.

Opportunity is everywhere even in punk rock.

"The cool thing about being famous is traveling.
I have always wanted to travel across seas, like to Canada and stuff."

—Britney Spears

ARE YOU STILL COOL?

Are you still cool? Are you making the same splash that you were making a year ago? Six months ago? Ever?

It's time to start asking yourself that question more often than not. The tides are changing so quickly that it is the companies that can ride the wave the smartest and fastest that will survive.

Here are some questions to ask yourself to see where you stand.

- Have you taken the time to rejuvenate your creative juices? How?
- Are you still working as hard as you did when you first started? Why or why not?
- Are you hiring the smartest, most versatile, creative thinkers that are currently hitting the work force?
- Are you in touch with your audience? What do you do to stay in touch?
- Are you pushing your industry forward or are you a follower?

Exercise: Give these questions out to the decision makers in your company and then reconvene for a discussion about your answers. I think you will be surprised by where each person thinks the company is at currently.

"4,950,000."

—The number of hits
that come up when
you do a Google
search for the word Buzz.

BZZAGENT MAPPLE REPORTING FOR DUTY, SIR

It could possibly be the most popular word in marketing and promotions and the only way to describe it is by using the word itself. Welcome to the world of *buzz.**

What is buzz? Buzz can best be described as what happens when people start talking about you and your product. This talk is honest and real. It's not street team marketers throwing samples in consumer's faces. Two people sitting around the water cooler talking about last night's episode of The Apprentice, now that's buzz.

Buzz is word of mouth exposure and it is powerful. It's a quick Instant Message from a friend on your buddy list about where she had dinner last night. It's not an unsolicited email from that restaurant.

Buzz will get you noticed by a large population of consumers. Don't get me wrong, email and sampling are important parts of getting your product known at the beginning of its lifecycle and once it is, buzz will take over. And when it does that is when you will know that you have something real on your hands.

**Become a fellow BzzAgent at www.bzzagent.com.*

*"You can't tell a kid that it's time to exercise; that's a turn-off…
you have to say 'Let's go to the park and have some fun."*

—Arnold Schwarzenegger

PICK UP THE PACE AND DON'T STOP UNTIL WE'RE DONE

Four times a week I teach cycling class at my local gym. Cycling, which is just one of the many names this activity goes under, is done on a stationary bicycle where you add or take away resistance to simulate uphill climbs or as most of the classes prefer, downhill sprints.

I teach at 6:30 in the morning. You probably wouldn't believe how many people are up at that hour exercising. I find it to be a great way to get the day going right off the bat.

The class begins promptly at 6:30 and lasts for one full hour. My goal is to not only get a great workout myself but to make it hard for the rest of the class. Yes, I am a punisher. You came to get a workout; by all means necessary you're going to get one.

When I first started teaching class participation was low. I'm talking about 2-5 students each time. It was a pitiful display of wasted space. Let's be honest here, they don't put those other 15 bikes in the room for decoration and I made it my mission to get butts in those seats ASAP.

Here's how I did it in less than two months. I made the best mix tapes with the best music on them and played them at a volume that would have made any heavy metal band blush. I always kept the door to the cycling room wide open when I taught and I turned down the lights so you could only see the shadows moving inside.

This caused two things to happen—new people started coming to my classes on a regular basis and they would get other gym members to attend as well. Why? Because I piqued their interest, they had to see what was going on and wanted to be a part of it. I created champions within the class. Two gentlemen in particular took it upon themselves to market my class to their workout group. My classes not only became a great place to "sweat to the oldies" but also a social hour.

"Never idealize others.
They will never live up to your expectations."

—Leo Buscaglia

GIVE THE PEOPLE WHAT THEY WANT

How many times have you gone to a concert only to be disappointed that the artist didn't play all of their big hits? I know I have.

Take Madonna who has a catalog of albums and has had songs on the pop charts for years. Some of the people in her audience have been with her since her first album while others may be just discovering her music for the first time. The lights go down and as Madonna makes her way to the stage the crowd goes crazy with anticipation. They are expecting "Holiday" or "Like A Virgin" to open the show. They'll even take "Vogue" and not complain. But when she comes out playing an acoustic number they are not going to be happy. Making things worse she might not do any of those songs tonight.

But can you really blame her for not wanting to sing "Like A Virgin," one more time? And is it really one more time? Not when you are on a 40 city tour it's not.

Have no fear, Madonna is not going to let us down. How could she? She's Madonna and we love her no matter what. Cleverly, planned or unplanned, Madonna is currently on her, get this, greatest hits tour! Now for the low price of $350 a ticket you can hear all of her hits in one perfect setting. No silly cover songs, no stupid banter with the audience, just the hits, just the way you like it. Happy?

Now Madonna isn't alone in this concert game and I don't mean to single her out. Check your ticket stubs for the Eagles, Prince, Phil Collins, Fleetwood Mac and a handful of others. But why complain, after all they are giving us exactly what we want and we are eating it up in droves.

"I'm not in this world to live up to your expectations
and you're not in this world to live up to mine."

—Bruce Lee

DON'T GIVE THE PEOPLE WHAT THEY WANT

I've got to hand it to the members of the rock band Phish. Just this week they announced after being together for over 20 years they are breaking up.

While I could care less for the tunes they play I've got to admire the way they are going out. Lead singer Trey Anastasio was quoted as saying that he just couldn't go on any more doing what he was doing. What was he doing? What he was doing was playing in Phish. One of the biggest grossing bands in today's music scene and he couldn't go on? Sold out shows months in advance, merchandise on every fan's back and a sticker on their car and he couldn't go on? There had to be something I was missing.

Anastasio cleared it all up when he went on to say something to the effect of, "how many times can I play "You Enjoy Yourself?" You see, "You Enjoy Yourself?" is one of those songs that the band probably played "a million" times. And while they were known for their different musical arrangements of their songs at their concerts, Anastasio hit the nail right on the head. Why continue doing something that you don't feel for anymore?

"Fame lost its appeal for me when I went into a public restroom and an autograph seeker handed me a pen and paper under the stall door."

—Marlo Thomas

DO YOU HAVE A PEN I CAN BORROW?

How many times have you heard that one during the day? Nothing drives me more crazy that that question by the way.

Get ready; I'm about to go off here. "Please, come on, take one of those cheap Bic pens that they always make you order at work and put it in your pocket! Now you will always have a pen and not only will you be the hero when someone asks for one but you will always be prepared when you need to jot down that award winning idea of yours." Thank you.

Ok, so you don't have to order one of those cheap pens from work because 99% of the businesses out there have already done it for you. I say start collecting them today. On Monday, be sure to take that free pen from Dr. Rush's chiropractic office. On Wednesday, grab that pen from the wicker basket on the counter when you drop off your dry cleaning at Wang's Dry Cleaning and Alterations off of 56th Avenue. And on Saturday, at that 5K you are running you can bet that the post race celebration is going to offer more than free Power Bars. Every sponsor at his or her table is going to have some tchotchke to give away, and I bet it will be a pen. These things are so cheap that if you don't have your own personalized pen, I question what you are waiting for.

Want to take this a step further? Than do what I do by making a game out of it. Start trading pens where ever you go. This game is so simple that you can play it without anyone else's participation. When I worked for the radio station, I would always have one of our pens in my bag. Whenever we went out for a meal I would sign the bill with the provided pen and replace it with the one from my bag.* How easy is that? Can you imagine how many people every day would now see our logo? And what did it cost the station for this free advertising? Well depending on how much we ate, virtually nothing.

**Just last night I returned to the restaurant and was waited on by a waiter I hadn't seen in awhile. When the bill was presented the pen inside was from the radio station I had worked for. I had left that same pen over 8 months ago.*

"Clothes make the man. Naked people have little or no influence on society."

—Mark Twain

YOU PAY FOR WHAT YOU GET

Thank you Ralph Lauren for my first white T-shirt and thank you Mom for putting up a fight and making me pay for it.

I was 15 years old and school was about to begin. With three kids my folks' clothing budget could be stretched very thin at times. This was one of those times and so we found ourselves at Marshall's for back to school clothes.

If you don't know what Marshall's is let me take a moment and tell you. Marshall's is one of those stores where you can find name brand clothing, even high end, at a budget price. Now I'm not talking about cheap, but a good value that beats the mall.

Well I wanted a white Polo brand T-shirt for some reason. To this day, I have no idea why I wanted it or if I even needed it. But I did and my mother wasn't going to pay for it. Why pay $22 for a basic white T when you could get one just like it for $9.99? Well the price difference was obvious; you were paying for that little embroidered horse. But to me it was much more than that.

I was paying for a better shirt that would outlast the $9.99 T by years. And you know what, it did. That Polo white T-shirt lasted throughout high school and college. The cotton material was outstanding and the little polo playing man logo stayed on even after hundreds of washings.

I am a firm believer in that you get what you pay for and this is where it all started for me.

"Any question—except "why"—is an inward journey that begins with: what, who, how, where and when."

—Larry James

I HEARD YOU LARRY JAMES

I was driving back to my apartment in Detroit from a long day spent in Cleveland, Ohio. It was late. I'm talking about 2 O'clock in the morning late.

My day was spent going to record stores and putting up displays on their walls for the latest and greatest artists on the pop charts. My job was to also talk these artists up to the managers in hope of receiving more in-store airplay thus resulting in sales. If a record is good, it works every time. And when a record sucks, you lie about it and hope to fool the manager. The latter, sadly, usually works every time as well!

This was a special road trip because after hitting 10 stores I would get to take a select group of retail employees backstage to meet Henry Rollins. Mr. Rollins, lead singer of the punk rock band Black Flag was now out on his own with the Rollins Band. They were promoting their first big album on a somewhat major label. Black Flag* and Henry Rollins are two of the artist that helped shaped my adolescence. They were a huge influence on my creativity and outlook on things around me. That's probably why I can't remember if I was more excited about the meet and greet than the 15 year old store clerks I was bringing back.

Hank, as I liked to call him, was one of those folks I admired for his strict code of ethics. If he said he was going to do something, he did. From running his own book publishing company to staying fit, Rollins is the man.

The Rollins Band is loud. They are one of those bands that after seeing them live you don't want to listen to anything else. I'm not talking about giving up all other bands; you just need some peace and quiet after an hour of musical assault from them. Lucky for me, I had a long drive in front of me and radio in this part of the country is nothing to cheer about.

As my drive reaches the halfway point, I can't take the silence anymore but the last thing I want to hear is a pounding bass or a wailing guitar. Enter, AM talk radio! The signal is terrible, the voices fade in and out and I can't make out how many programs I am really listening to since the static is overwhelming. Then suddenly I hear the voice of Larry James. He is being interviewed about his book, *How To Really Love The One You're With.*** The book sounds amazing and like one I must pick up as soon as Borders opens tomorrow morning.

"The radio of my youth…is now a quaint memory
replaced by a computer hard drive."

—Talk show host Phil Donahue

James wrote the book for himself and after passing it around to a few friends the feedback was so overwhelmingly positive he just had to share it with the world. I'm glad he did. Larry's book moved me so much that I called him after finishing it. He wasn't in but I left a message and within 15 minutes my phone rang. It was Larry James on the line.

He didn't have to call me back. But he did and I will never forget it.

**Be sure to pick up Black Flag's Who's Got The 10 ½ album to see what I mean.*

***James' book is still in print and highly recommended.*

*"Surfing on the Internet is like sex;
everyone boats about doing more than they
actually do.
But in the case of the Internet, it's a lot
more."*

—Tom Fasulo

GET PHATZ

While on one hand I can't get enough of the World Wide Web and what it has to offer there was a time when I would call it the World Wide Waste and really meant it. While my Pay Pal account was heavily in use, I really had nothing to show for my countless hours of surfing no matter how hard I tried.

Despite that fact, I still today find myself surfing along the information highway at top DSL speed but now I'm highly selective on where my Netscape browser points. One site that has garnered my attention more often than not is www.phatz.com. The philosophy behind Phatz* is clearly stated on their home page and is something that every web designer should print out and tape to their monitor.

Gone are the days of blinking buttons and goofy gadgets. Our team focuses on the intellectual approach, creating functional, useful web sites that are lightning fast, content focused and visually appealing. No gadgets. No junk code. No useless functionality....just: 100% ultra clean design.

Wow! How much better would the World Wide Web be if every website followed the above mantra of straight forward and appealing pages? What are you doing to make your customer's web experience simple?

**I landed on Phatz not through a search engine or from a random link or from a friend suggesting it, Phatz came to me one day as I drove behind Christian (I actually think it was his girlfriend's car and he was in the passenger seat) who runs Phatz. He loudly proclaims the website on the rear and side windows. Stop reading and go to his site now and check out his photos and clever essays.*

"It rubs me the wrong way, a camera…
It's a frightening thing."

—Bob Dylan

SMILE YOU'RE ON CANDID CAMERA

Digital cameras are everywhere. Walk in to your local Best Buy and there are dozens of choices to choose from. Go to CVS to pick up your prescription and you can pick up a disposable digital camera for a few extra bucks. These things have gotten so cheap that if you don't have one you are in the minority. There really is no excuse not to have one. The latest kind to hit the market comes included in your cell phone.

With the proliferation of digital cameras and cell phones what is a marketer to do to make sure his product is the one leaving those shelves? Let's take a look at what Sony Ericsson did to launch their Sony T68i cell phone camera.

They hired a 120 person street team that would hang out in tourist hot spots like Times Square or the Space Needle in Seattle and ask people to take their picture using their Sony Ericsson T68i phone. What a great way to get their product in the hands of people in the ideal setting. This simple little "trick" was a conversation starter that had people talking and using the phone/camera without them knowing that they were being marketed to.

Did this promotion work? You bet it did. Not only was the phone covered in the New York Times and on CNBC but it also created a waiting list to get one of these hot new items.

Way to go Sony Ericsson!

"I believe in looking reality straight in the eye and denying it."

—Garrison Keillor

HUMAN INTERACTION FOR SALE

With the Sony Ericsson cell phone/camera example in mind, are you familiar with the term "leaner?"

A leaner is a good-looking employee paid by a company who infiltrates your settings without you even knowing it. A leaner will walk into a crowded bar and order a drink made by the company who hired him. They will casually start a conversation with the people around them expounding on the merits of the product. It seems so causal that no one would ever expect it to be a marketing "trick."

How about this marketing tool that is being applied at a bar near you? An advertising company hires a group of friends to hang out in a bar and have them all order the same drink. At any one time, the product can be seen from any angle in the bar because the group has been hired to make sure that it is that way. The idea is to show the popularity of the product and how it is readily available right now.

Here's one even better than that, a marketing firm was hired by a catalog company to promote its mail order business. When you placed an order with the company your package would arrive in 3-5 days in a box that displayed the company's logo on all sides. The campaign the marketing company designed was one that would showcase the popularity of the company, or should I say the implied popularity. The marketing company paid doormen at business and residential buildings to leave packages at their desks so it would look like orders had been delivered but hadn't been picked up yet.

So what's real anymore? Nothing.*

**I just heard Paris Hilton, star of the reality show Simple Life, admit that she was acting in most scenes for the laughs and the ratings benefit. Now that's reality TV for you!*

"I'm not computer literate. I email. I know how to get on the Web, but I haven't crossed over into the Internet world. I'm old-fashioned, I guess."

—Katie Holmes

WHAT'S YOUR EMAIL ADDRESS?

Does anyone stop and actually write a letter anymore? By this I mean, sit down at a desk, take out a piece of paper and put pen to paper. The once considered art form is fading fast as email becomes the number one way people correspond with each other.

If you do not have some type of email communication with your customers, whether they be current or potential you are missing out on a huge opportunity. In a 2001 Forrester survey, 92% of the respondents said email is more effective in maintaining loyalty than in acquiring customers. Keep in mind that it costs a lot more to acquire a new customer than it does to keep one. Once you have shown and demonstrated your product is a value worthy to a customer they are practically yours. So, how are you going to keep them?

Email can be the easiest, most cost effective way to reach your customers. This is your key to open the door to customer loyalty. Don't let the door close on you. Start an email database and reach out to your fans now.

Email can not only promote your product but it can be used as a valuable market research tool. Ask your customers for feedback and offer incentives for their honest opinions. Make your emails entertaining with contests that are simple to win and be sure to spotlight the winners in the next mailing. Showcase your fans like the stars that they are.

There are a few rules to all of this, don't barrage your customer's email account. Mailings should go out twice a month if warranted but never more. Keep them informed and excited about you and they will stay happy. Make sure you give them the option to forward your email on to their friends as well. And be sure to give them a handy "print me" icon for those that want to take your email with them. Make things simple and you will see your efforts go a long way.

"I'm tired of hearing about money, money, money, money, money, money, money. I just want to play the game, drink Pepsi, wear Reebok."

—Shaquille O'Neal

THIRSTY?

We've all seen those commercials for Pepsi that take a blatant slam at Coca Cola. I've got to admit they are pretty damn funny. The one with the Pepsi truck that's been pimped out is a classic. And no one can forget the one with the Coke delivery driver who can't overcome his desire for a Pepsi and he has to sneak one while on the job.

Last night I saw the latest Pepsi slam and it got me thinking The commercial shows a young kid walking down the street with a pocket full of change. The setting is the early 60s and the heat is on. It's the dead of summer and it is so hot out that the street is steaming. Our young star has a decision to make, Coke or Pepsi?

Of course he chooses Pepsi.

Conveniently the Pepsi vending machine is right outside of a guitar store. As the young man takes the first sip of his ice cold Pepsi, a Jimi Hendrix tune begins to play furiously by a solo guitar and we are shown that the young boy is in fact Jimi Hendrix at age 12. Across the street, we see the lonely Coke vending machine outside of a dusty old antique store and the song plays again this time by a boring old accordion.

I've got to admit that this commercial is pretty good. With all of the clutter on the TV now-a-days Pepsi got me to laugh and it was out loud. Even so that wasn't enough to make me reach for a Pepsi anytime soon. But why?

Will this commercial make me drink more Pepsi? Probably not. What it does is reinforce the spirit of Pepsi as the underdog. Coke is the leader in this category no matter how funny or smart Pepsi's advertising is.

Which product do you relate to?

"One martini is all right.
Two are too many,
and three are not enough."

—James Thurber

SHAKEN NOT STIRRED

Musical trends are like the restaurant business. At any moment your fifteen minutes could be up. On Wednesday, the food critic for the hip free weekly is saying you have the best fish tacos in town and by the next issue he's already found somewhere better. It might not be fair but that's the way it is.

In the music business it's not much better. MTV, *Spin* magazine and those folks at *Entertainment Weekly* could be hailing you one week as the new singer/songwriter sensation to take the crown from Bob Dylan followed by never being mentioned again. Or even worse you are being hailed as the band that will save the genre from its own demise. Call yourself Limp Bizkit, Metallica or Norah Jones it doesn't really matter.

Every few weeks, it seems the cycle happens and we the public are thrown another new musical sensation. Sometimes it's a new artist and other times it's a whole new movement. Whatever the case, you can be sure that it is not by accident that all of the sudden you can't escape the latest and greatest.

Bored with rock? Sick of that driving techno beat? The Rolling Stones and Neil Young sounding too much like your father's music? Have no fear, because here comes the latest craze circling the nation. Here's how it happens. It usually starts in the back room of some college kid's dorm and immediately spreads to all of his hip friends that we will call "influencers." These influencers will start to spread the news to all of their hip friends. Some of these friends will be artists, filmmakers, writers and the like. And before you know it the experiment to try to create something new has spread. It's spreading so fast you can no longer tell who started it in the first place. And within months, your parents will know who your new favorite band is. They'll be on Regis and Kelly so set your VCR, if you dare. Sad but true.

Take lounge music for instance. Yes believe it or not there was a time when this (old) new music was sweeping the nation. Hipsters were dressing like their grandparents once did. The music was alive again and the bars were full.

"I don't believe in having bands for solo records."

—Mick Jagger

Everyone, like it or not, was almost required to have a martini in one hand and a cigar in the other. A Cuban exile led the way as the genre's grand marshall and no one cared when the music originally came out. Cocktail hour had begun and nothing was going to stop it. Well, except for the next hip movement to take over.

"I never drink water; that is the stuff that rusts pipes."

—W. C. Fields

SHAKEN NOT STIRRED (PART 2)

The movement lasted long enough for me to find a quick way to make a buck off of it. First, let me say, I really liked the music and the names and the records were not that new to me. The drinking of top shelf liquors and the hunt for a really great cigar suited me perfectly. While the music might not be hip anymore, these two characteristics of the fad live on. Well at least with my palate.

Shaken Not Stirred was the name of my magazine that tried to capture the lounge music scene through words and pictures. I had set out to visually describe what was taking place in the scene at the time. The movement was at its peak and you could almost see the end coming but I had a hunch it was far enough off so why not print something up. I wanted to give readers something that they could take home and share. It didn't matter what part of the lounge wave they were riding. If you were in because of the tunes, I had it covered. If the lifestyle and look was your thing, *Shaken Not Stirred* was here to help. The magazine was printed on flourescent color paper so it stood out and you knew you were reading something different. Something that spoke to you in a way that *Spin* or *Rolling Stone* wasn't going to be able to do about the same subject matter.

The articles on the different types of cigars went into detail about each type of stogie and had points that even the most seasoned smoker could pick up. I interviewed the woman that put together the Rhino Records box set on lounge music and she was more than happy to talk to me. So much so she was the focal point of an issue. Which shouldn't be that much of a surprise, because the genre, fashion influences aside, was about the music. The rest of the magazine was filled with record reviews and some drink recipes.

Once the first issue was produced all I had to do was get the word out about it. How was I going to do that? Simple, repeat after me, "the Internet is your friend." In these situations it can be a life saver. A quick search revealed that Yahoo! Groups was pretty active with other lounge enthusiasts. A few message board postings about *Shaken Not Stirred* got the ball rolling. Another search for websites was the kick I needed. Type in lounge music or one of the many artists' names and a list of websites would be displayed. For a week I would contact the webmasters of these sites and in exchange for a review of *Shaken Not Stirred* I would review their website in an upcoming issue. A perfect trade for all involved.

"Don't play what's there, play what's not there."

—Miles Davis

That was the easy part. How was I going to get some stranger to send a few bucks to a PO Box in Atlanta, Georgia? Easy, tempt them with a "secret surprise inside." That was my gimmick. Every issue came with a FREE gift. It was just enough of an incentive to make you spend your money in the hope of getting something back that was more than worth it. The surprise was a printed up drink recipe and a colorful drink umbrella. Within weeks my PO Box was filled to the brim. Requests were coming in from all over the world; you can thank the Internet for that.

"A man is hit by a car while crossing a
Beverly Hills street.
A woman rushes to him and cradles his
head in her lap,
asking, "Are you comfortable?"
The man answers, "I make a nice living."

—Milton Berle

THE BUG AND THE HUM VEE

Yesterday I took a drive around the busiest section of the city. What I found was not surprising. I'm guessing that I could have done this same exercise in your town with the same results. What did I find?

Coming out of the back alleys and onto the big streets of marketing and promotions, is the VW Bug and the Hummer H2. These two extremes are the biggest (and the smallest) things to grab the attention of business owners who want to take their message to the street with a moving billboard. Can you blame them? Can you pass one of these cars without looking at it even though you've seen one hundreds of times?

The VW Bug* is making a huge comeback and the new convertible model is an eye catcher from a mile away. The Bug could quite possibly be the perfect marketing vehicle. I've seen them morphed into a mouse with a tail and whiskers. Delta Airlines has a fleet of them that look like mini airplanes. On the streets of Orlando you can see Shamu, the killer whale from Sea World as portrayed by a handful of carefully decorated Bugs. Just yesterday I saw a local travel agency advertise its services with a Bug that had been wrapped with a map of the world. Did they ever get their message across on what they do!

If the Bug is the perfect marketing vehicle then the Hummer H2 is its close cousin. Taking it to the extreme the H2 is the monster of real street marketing. While I haven't seen one morphed into an animal or wrapped to resemble anything other than what it is, the H2 does get noticed no matter what's going on. How can you not notice the biggest gas-guzzler on the road today? Marketers are putting their message on the enormous back window and side windows. Wrap your message on the side doors and the next thing you know is your message is at eye level with any passing car.

While the cost difference between the two can be incredible, you're paying for size. Mobile marketing—big or small—is a great way to get your message out when and where people least expect it.

**The Punch Bug game is one of my childhood favorites. You'll need two or more people to play. When the first person in your party spots a Bug they say Punch Bug and politely punch the person next to them in the arm.*

"If you don't mind smelling like peanut butter
for two or three days,
peanut butter is darn good shaving cream."

—Barry Goldwater

SHAVE YOUR FACE WITH THIS

I am currently in the middle of doing a market research study for a new men's razor. My task is to shave for two weeks with the product and report back via a written log. Once completed, I will be given another razor and do the same thing over again. Why am I doing this? Because it's a great way to have a small part in the launch of a new product before it hits the retail shelves.

This isn't the first time I have been involved in market research of this kind. I have watched pilots for TV shows, drank low carb beer, watched commercials for hotel chains and chewed tobacco among many other things. Sometimes they are solo projects like the razor study and other times you are in a room with ten other people discussing the topic.

What I have found is that this type of market research is still one of the best ways to garner feedback about your product. Whether you're selling razors, providing a service or have come up with a new chocolate brownie mix. Getting your potential audience to talk candidly about your product can be beneficial. I recommend it for any company no matter how big or small.

Make sure you are taking the time and effort to receive honest feedback about what it is you are doing. Set up your own market research studies and do them as often as needed. Create an open and comfortable setting for your guests. Offer snacks, a light dinner or some sort of monetary incentive. Even something as small as a tour of your facility can have value. The incentive doesn't have to cost you a lot but you can be sure that in the mind of your customer it will be thought of as something worth "millions" and only obtainable to the very lucky few. This will be one of the keys to your success.

"Far and away the best prize that life has
to offer
is the chance to work hard at work worth
doing."

—Theodore Roosevelt

CUSTOMER SERVICE IS JOB ONE

Ask any sales rep that sells tchotchkes about me and they will tell you that I am tough to deal with. When I say, tough I don't mean in a jerky way, I mean that I know what I want and I know what I should be paying for it. Everything has a mark-up and I am more than willing to keep the economy going, but at the same time I will not be taken advantage of. Because of that, I am also one of the nicest people to deal with because I understand what it takes to make a sale and appreciate the people that do the selling.

With that knowledge, take a look at this situation; I typically buy my tchotchke items from one seller and one seller only. I have followed this rule for over 15 years. I not only do this to simplify my buying process but it ensures that I establish a close relationship with the seller and his company. Remember, in the end, it really is all about your relationships and here's how I know that to be true.

We were doing a major promotion that I knew was going to receive not only newspaper coverage but also TV. This event is a big deal in Atlanta and people look forward to it each year. Three days before the event I received a call from CNN that they would be covering the event. I needed to capitalize on this national exposure immediately. But what could I do with such short notice?

Obviously I panicked first and then came up with an idea. I wanted to dress my staff up in bright blue shirts with our logo printed on them as big as possible. You would be able to tell where we were from a mile away. But that wasn't all I wanted to do. I wanted to outfit the first half of the line at the event. These were the hardcore fans that the TV cameras and newspaper photographers were going to capture.

I placed a phone call to my merchandise representative and after some initial shock about what I was seeking we had a plan. He would push my special-last-minute order to the front of the line. We would be able to get this done but everything would take place right up to the last second. My shirts would be printed as soon as I signed off on a proof, which would take a day for me to see. We were up against the wall but we knew that we could get the job done.

"The fragrance always remains on the hand that gives the rose."

—Gandhi

The proof arrived and as luck would have it the font I wanted was not right. Back to the drawing board it went and we lost half a day. Now we were really cutting it close. A little too close for my comfort but I never gave up thinking we were not going to get this done.

The new proof arrived and with a quick sign off we were off to the printers. Now here's where it gets tricky. Once the shirts were done, they would be overnighted to me. My event started at 5:30 in the morning and I now had a choice to make. The choices were the shirts could arrive at 3 O'clock in the morning or at 5. I couldn't take the chance of the shirts not being here so I chose 3AM gambling that if they didn't get on that flight I could still make the 5AM arrival and pull off my plan. Luckily, my relationship was strong with my merchandise rep because here's where customer service came in to play.

Someone had to go get those shirts at the airport in the middle of the night. Guess what? My merchandise rep said he would do it and he would deliver them to my house. Talk about customer service! This was totally unexpected but it guaranteed that he would receive my business for years to come.

What have you done today to guarantee business for the years ahead of you?

"You can't be a real country unless you have a beer and an airline. It helps if you have some kind of a football team, or some nuclear weapons, but at the very least you need a beer."

—Frank Zappa

BANDS LOVE BEER!

Make no mistake about it musicians love beer. In fact the only thing they like better is free beer. And the only thing they like better than free beer is the fact that their name and album title is printed on the bottle.

Believe it or not, there was a time when a great beer was hard to find. Now some of you Budweiser purists are probably squirming in your seats but give me a moment here please. What I'm saying is that there was a time when you couldn't find a great micro-beer at just any old restaurant you pleased. Thus, some folks decided that brewing their own beer at home would be a wise choice.

I'm one of those folks. Why not? You get to pick your flavor, buy the ingredients, let it stink up your house as you boiled the mixture and watch it ferment all in one afternoon. While I wasn't giving Sam Adams and Pete's anything to worry about, it was the experience that made the difference.

It wasn't easy but we're not talking rocket science either. Ok, there is some science involved but it's only beer after all, which explains why one out of every few batches I brewed was just awful. But I digress, after a few successful attempts word got out about my beer making science project. So much so, that my favorite local band asked if I wouldn't mind brewing the beer for their CD release party. Would I? You bet I would!

I brewed a special ale in honor of the band and was sure that everything was done right. From the ingredients to the bottles that housed it, this was my best brew ever. And it was. You might even say, "delicious!"

The best thing I liked about the project was designing the labels for the bottles. I used the band's logo, their album artwork along with the made up brewery I had created. It was beautiful. Maybe too beautiful, because as I looked around the room no one was drinking them! A few girls had them hanging out of their purses. A few guys had them in their back pocket, unopened I might add. And a group of mothers were getting them autographed by their sons.

I guess, sometimes it's not what's inside that counts but how it looks from the outside that makes the real difference in people's lives.

"Discipline is the soul of an army.
It makes small numbers formidable;
procures success to the weak, and esteem to all."

—George Washington

A ONE MAN TEAM CAN WIN WITH THE RIGHT ATTITUDE

Recently I attended a sold out pop music concert that had every local radio station outside the arena doing their thing. Some were broadcasting live with a full mobile studio, another was merely there for presence and one was just standing there.

The latter was just plain pathetic and we'll get back to them in a moment. The others came with a mission and were completing it. They were meeting their listeners and taking care of them. Each one was playing their station at a volume that drowned out the next. They were standing in brightly colored logoed tents and people were walking away with station T-shirts, bumper stickers and key chains. Their listeners all had smiles on their faces and were talking to each other about the station and the DJ they just met. The radio station staff that was working the event seemed to be having a great time as well. The excitement they created was reminiscent of a carnival or a birthday party. If you asked some of the many fans in attendance, they might say that the concert was an added bonus at this point of the night

Now back to that other station, boy were they a sad looking sight. They arrived after the other stations putting them at a disadvantage. All the good spots in front of the venue were taken and any hope of getting a parking spot where their logo could be seen was nonexistent. You could say they were SOL!

Sheepishly the one lone employee got out of the station vehicle and surveyed what was left for the taking. He found a spot and proceeded to set up a table. No wait, he wasn't going to really set it up, he was going to use it as a seat. And sit he did for over 45 minutes while the controlled chaos went on around him, waiting for his team to show up. What an embarrassment it was. I kind of even felt bad for him. He sat there reading the sports section, in a station branded T-shirt and looked like a complete idiot!

I wasn't the only one to notice. One of the more creative stations was bribing listeners with free station gear if they would walk over to the guy and have their picture taken with him behind his back while holding a station banner. This station managed to bury their competition, get a few laughs with some of their listeners and boost the morale of those working the event.

"Be all that you can be."

—United States Army slogan

But was he really SOL?

I don't think so. Did he give up? Sure, but for no reason. Even though he was faced with many hurdles he could have done something. Set up the table and put the table skirt on it. Start meeting your listeners and handing out your station items. Build a crowd around you, because the number one rule to follow in this situation is that nothing attracts a crowd like a crowd. He needed to do something, anything, but instead he chose not to.

"If you don't watch where you are going, you might end up someplace else."

—Yogi Berra

WHERE ARE YOU HEADED?

As a leader of a brand you must stay focused at all times. While that might sound simple in theory, it is a task that can easily be forgotten. Our daily work schedule gets clouded and confusing as the day goes on. We start the day fresh even though the pile of work from yesterday is front and center on our desk. We catch up all day by putting more projects in the stack. How are we ever expected to know where we are going except into another long workday that won't end at five o'clock?

One-way of finding out where you are headed is by maintaining a strong brand at all times. Following these suggestions will set you on a path that will keep you focused on what you have set out to create.

- Focus on whom you are trying to reach. Don't get confused.
- Know your message. Make it straightforward and clear.
- Take a chance. It's said all too often because it is true, step outside the box (or bun).
- Stay with your goal for however long it takes. Do not give up!
- If you say that you are going to do something, do it.
- Keep your message front and center when you talk to your consumers. Remind them why they chose you in the first place.
- Don't be afraid to spend money to support your brand but do spend it smart.
- Check yourself. Is your brand still important to your customers?
- Following is great but be a leader. Encourage others to step up to the plate.

"Surgeon General's Warning: Smoking Causes Lung Cancer, Heart Disease, Emphysema, and May Complicate Pregnancy."

—United States Surgeon General

THROWING UP MARLBORO RED

Go out to any bar in your town tonight and when you walk in take a look around. It doesn't have to be a long look but one that's just long enough for you to see all the signage that hangs from the ceiling and is stapled to the walls.

Now close your eyes and say out loud the name of three beer companies and one cigarette company that "own" this bar. It should be a pretty easy exercise. These companies spend more money than you can imagine on signage. And for one year I was a part of this money-spending machine.

I was the Local Promotions Manager for the Marlboro Bar Program in Atlanta. What a great job this was. I got to work with a younger staff that was not only fun to be around but also one that was eager to learn what we were doing.

My Marlboro adventure started with two long days of training in Philadelphia in one of those big hotel conference rooms. At the front of the room were two large screen projectors, a podium and a table stacked high with Marlboro Reds, Lights and Menthols. In the air hung a thick cloud of smoke produced by the 300 trainees that sat patiently listening to the directors talk.

Marlboro training school taught me something very important. Something so important in the field of marketing and promotions that I make it a mandatory lesson for my entire staff and now I am going to share it with you.

Let's go back to our exercise at the beginning of this chapter; can you still recall the company's names? It shouldn't be too hard to do. The lesson I learned was that every event we did—it better look like someone threw up Marlboro red all over the place. How simple is that? Wherever you look the patrons better know that they have entered Marlboro country. The "M" logo is the focus point and it should be seen from all angles.

This simple rule can apply to your product and is easy to test at your events. Just do the exercise over and over until you own the place!

"I've heard snappier comebacks from a bowl of Rice Krispies."

—Charles Emerson Winchester III

SAMPLE THIS!

One hot summer I thought it would be a good idea to do some sample-based marketing. Sample-based marketing is where you give away free samples of your product in hopes that it will lead to a sale down the line. I was eager to learn this side of the business mostly because I enjoy the direct contact with the public. Sampling allows you to receive direct feedback from your consumers on many levels. Besides who doesn't like something for free?

My project was the new chocolate flavored Rice Krispy Treats. Mmmmm, delicious and who could turn them down? I'll tell you, no one it turns out can, because the cases and cases of product I had in the warehouse disappeared in no time.

We gave away these Treats at sporting events, the park on the weekend and as conventioneers were walking back to their hotel downtown. Everyone wanted one to eat now and one for later. This went on for the entire month of August.

The hook to the whole promotion was that each sample had a $1.00 off coupon attached to it. Not only were you receiving a free sample but also you had the opportunity to purchase a box at a discount. But here's the kicker to the whole story, the bars were not available yet anywhere in the metro area.

Thousands of people had tried the product and liked it. These individuals all had coupons in their hand they were ready to use and try to use them they did. The consumer help line that was printed on the coupon received complaints that the product couldn't be found. Grocery store managers were asked to stock the product as soon as they could. We had created market frenzy for a product that people wanted but wasn't available. By November, Rice Krispy Treats were flying off the shelves of grocery stores and ensured that our marketing and promotional goals had been met.

"Well, I'm playing for the fans so whenever they come and ask for autographs I always try to give it to everybody because I'm out there for the people."

—Anna Kournikova

I'M YOUR BIGGEST FAN

To survive in any business you need an army to support you. This army will be made up of your biggest fans. And you better treat them with the highest regard because they are worth it, tenfold.

This core group will be made up of the many different demographics that support your product but there will be three things that will separate them from your other fans.

1) They will spread the word about you to everyone they know. This can be in conversation, by wearing your gear or through the many outlets on the Internet including personal web pages, chat rooms and message boards.

2) They will tell you without asking what they like and what they don't like about what you are doing. You won't need to solicit them for instant feedback because they will give it to you immediately. Take what they say seriously and respond accordingly. Get to know them by name and call them often.

3) They will stand up for you when others talk bad and they will defend your actions. After all they are an army and they will fight to the death for what they believe in. They believe in you!

Stacy: "Happy anniversary, Wayne."
Wayne: "Stacy, we broke up two months ago."
Stacy: "Well, that doesn't mean we can't still go out, does it?"
Wayne: "Well, it does actually, that's what breaking up is."

—From the movie *Wayne's World*

BURN THIS!

A few years back I was introduced to the mainly West Coast festival phenomenon called Burning Man. If you are not familiar with this one of a kind event, let me take a moment to fill you in.

Burning Man is the ultimate forum for free expression. It is where you can be whatever you want to be for one week with the hope that what you bring to it might leave with you. When Larry Harvey's girlfriend broke up with him he needed some self-therapy in the form of creating a wooded man that represented the person his girlfriend had left him for. What he did with that man has touched thousands of people—he lit it on fire on the beach!

It was Labor Day weekend and this shameless act created a tradition. The first time it was Larry and a handful of friends, the next year the group grew and when I went it was no longer on that beach and there were over a thousand people there.

The event is now held in the temporary city of Black Rock, outside of Reno and is a yearly weeklong event. There is no commerce except for the price of admission (it starts around $100 and goes up as the event gets closer), what you bring in is what you survive on and you are encouraged to let your freak flag fly. Self expression is a must at Burning Man and if you are not participating you have the chance of not only being in the minority but also being left out of some amazing things.

Throughout the week each camp (you meet people and form camps within the city) builds simple to elaborate works of art. At Burning Man art is in the eye of the beholder—you'll see everything from one act plays on makeshift stages to swing sets that will have you fifty feet in the air. Nothing is impossible at Burning Man and people spend money to create like it is going out of style.*

At the end of the week, all gather around the man which is no longer a small figure but one that stands high in the air graced by neon lights and balls that blaze fire all around him. At the stroke of midnight, the man's arms raise and with a single spark he is set ablaze. The crowd goes wild, dancing and cheering begins and the celebration continues in every camp. If you created a stage to

"How to avoid death and dismemberment in Black Rock…"

—From *The Burning Man Survival Guide*

perform on, you set it on fire. If you made a model for the other city dwellers to walk through, you set it afire. The nature of the event becomes not only symbolic but also religious in a way. One ritual is to cast all of your belongings into the fire around the Man, symbolizing not only that the festival has come to an end but also you are leaving behind a bit of what you brought with you. Having done this I can only say that it not only takes a weight off your shoulder but it comes about as a huge relief to your conscience.

**Check out www.burningman.com for more details about the festival to see some amazing pictures of the man and the many camps and faces that make up this unique festival.*

"It's hard to take over the world when you sleep 20 hours a day."

—From the comic strip *Get Fuzzy*

CLAIM YOUR SPACE

Are you familiar with the recent flash mob phenomenon? A flash mob is when a group of people take over an un-suspecting place and act out some sort of art. The art can be a political speech, a one-minute sonnet or anything that will grab the attention of those standing around.

The idea has become so popular that it is picking up steam and taking hold of urban trendsetters who have started to call it "space hijacking." So, what is space hijacking? It's the next logical step in the process whereby hijackers are searching out spaces that will actually attract people to them.

Recent space hijackings have taken place on an elevated train track in New York, a subway car (while in service), and my personal favorite, a fashion show that took place at a Wal-Mart located in a small outskirts town of Georgia.

Why are flash mobs and space hijacking becoming so popular? Because we are constantly looking out for something different from the way we have been doing things.

The landscape is changing, literally.

*"If a million people see my movie,
I hope they see a million different movies."*

—Quentin Tarantino, referring to his movie *Pulp Fiction*

WHY NETFLIX WORKS

Do you know how Reed Hastings got the idea for Netflix? He was pissed off at paying his Blockbuster late fees. Can you blame him?

Isn't it crazy that those late fees we all hate are a big part of the Blockbuster business model? Now I understand you only have yourself to blame when they occur but do you know anyone that walks away smiling when they have to pay them? I don't.

On the way to the gym after paying his "fine," Hastings started to think about the business model of the gym he was about to enter. Like most gyms, Hastings paid a monthly fee for unlimited workouts. Could the same model be structured for movie rentals? Of course it can and it's in place right now with Hastings' Netflix leading the way.

But why does it work? The obvious is the convenience it creates for consumers. What might not be so obvious to you is the fact that the DVD was and is the perfect product for this online rental business. They fit nicely in a padded envelope something a VHS tape would never get away with. Where Netflix kicks serious butt is that you get to keep the movie as long as you like while only paying a monthly fee. Late fee problem solved. But how long can this model stay profitable with the expansion of new technology? I'm not sure now that movies on demand isn't that far off in to the future.

This is why Netflix is already talking about debuting its movies on demand service next year. RealNetworks and Movielink aren't that far behind either. And if you think TiVo is not going to be a big part of this, you're wrong.

Blockbuster's earnings are expected to fall ten percent this year while Netflix has had 80% growth each year its been around and is currently at the two million customer level.

How we view movies at home is changing rapidly. It might be time to invest in a home theater system after all.

"All of the books in the world contain no more information than is broadcast on video in a single large American city in a single year.
Not all bits have equal value."

—Carl Sagan

SIGN OF THE TIMES

It used to be you would run a TV commercial or a newspaper ad to get the word out about your grand opening or event. Then came direct mail or simply putting flyers on cars. Next up we have email announcements and the like. But the coolest thing I have seen lately is the video vest.

The video vest or the T-shirt TV as it is being called is being utilized by the movie studios right now as the latest strategy in letting you know about their movies. Street teams are hitting the parks, shopping malls and anywhere else a crowd is gathered with vests that have a flat screen monitor dead center on their chest. They even play sound.*

How cool is that? Very. You can't get past these people without at least taking the slightest look to see what it is and if the trailer is creative enough you'll have an audience surrounding you in no time.

**If the T-shirt TV is in your price range be sure to check out the manufactured Aver-Wear who is currently the only maker of such an item that I know of. If the video vest is out of your budget check out the newest in backpacks that let you play a CD or a digital media player through their built-in speakers. While not as effective it will create a stir when you walk down the block.*

"I want a guy who can play 36 holes of golf,
and still have enough energy to take
Warren and me to a baseball game, and
eat sausages, and beer,
not Lite beer, but beer.
That's my ad, print it up."

—Mary from the movie, *There's Something About Mary*

OLD NEWS IS STILL OLD NEWS

It takes a lot to get me to react to a new product and even more to impress me, so when I saw the digital newspaper kiosk stand at the airport last week it stopped me in my tracks.

If you haven't seen one yet it is *almost* worth the trip to the airport alone. Note, I said almost and that is because I was highly disappointed with what I received not what I saw.

What I saw was for five dollars instantly billed to my credit card I could get a print out of a newspaper from practically anywhere in the world. There was the *New York Times*, the *Daily Telegraph* from England and one from China that I have no idea how to pronounce to name just a few. I couldn't stop staring at the machine and what it was saying it could accomplish and I wasn't alone judging by the crowd of people that started to gather behind me.

I chose the New York Times and watched as the screen produced an icon that looked like a piece of paper that soon traveled across the screen to the "just printed" side. In minutes I would have today's *Times*, or so I thought.

What came out of the machine looked beautiful—nice white paper, full sized like the *Times* and stapled like a report, three times. What didn't look so good was the date of the paper. It was 5 days old!

What a disappointment! Nowhere did the machine advertise this. I had been ripped off in the biggest possible way and to make matters worse no one at the counter could help me. But my trouble didn't end there.

When I arrived home from my vacation, I tried calling the company that owns the machine and would you believe that their number is no longer in service? I wonder why.

"Pop is actually my least favorite kind of music,
because it lacks real depth."

—Christina Aguilera

TOP OF THE POPS

I'm not sure how it started but I know that it is a habit that I haven't broken for over 10 years. Every year, I keep a list of the records that made an impact on me over the last 365 days. My list is called Top of the Pops and it is always close by. Ask me what my number one record was in 2001 and I'll tell you it was the Old 97s. In 2000 it was the Pinehurst Kids. The same goes for any other year.*

Why make a list like this? "Why not," I ask? I have a friend that records every movie he sees in his PDA and then writes a review to read at a later date. One guy I know keeps an overly detailed report on each bottle of wine he consumes. Another likes to keep track of her meals every time she goes to a restaurant. Why? I have no idea and I don't ask. We all keep some sort of list for our own enjoyment.

Recently, I gave my grandmother a book called "Family History." This is no ordinary book. Although each page comes with some direction for the most part the pages are completely blank until written in. At the top of each page, a thought provoking question is asked. The questions range from topics such as life in the depression to our family tree. My hope is that the book will last through many generations and be passed down through the ages.

This simple task is so important and I encourage you to do the same. Stories are what make us. Without them we are nothing. Do not be afraid to share your stories however big or small. From what you did last night to your best family vacation. Go tell someone. Do it now!

**In 2003 Massive Attack's 100 Years was my number one record. What makes it interesting is that they have been around for years and this is the first time I have been exposed to them. Who does their marketing?*

"Making coffee has become the great compromise of the decade. It's the only thing "real" men do that doesn't seem to threaten their masculinity.
To women, it's on the same domestic entry level as putting the spring back into the toilet-tissue holder or taking a chicken out of the freezer to thaw."

—Erma Bombeck

BEER AND COFFEE SNOBS UNITE

They say that rules are meant to be broken and I will tell you that I have one rule that I will not break and I don't care how thirsty I am. I will not drink any mass produced beer and I will not drink any coffee that doesn't come with some ridiculous price tag attached.

Say what you want about me but I have my standards. There is no such thing as all things being equal. You cannot compare a can of Bud Light with a pint of Grant's IPA. You just can't and I won't hear otherwise. Now have you heard of Grant's Brewery? Most likely not and that's fine with me. The biggest reason you probably haven't heard of this exceptional Northwest brewery is that they don't do much advertising and zero on the national scale. On the other hand you can't escape the Bud Light girls or any of their silly commercials—Spuds Mackenzie included. So which beer is better? If we compare it by gallons sold the race is undisputed. If we count it by brand recognition Bud Light slams Grant's into the ground. But how many people do you know that get excited when they see Bud Light on the menu? Not many I would imagine. Then there are those people that get really excited and start smiling when they talk about their favorite beer? This is the type of person I want to sit next to at the bar. This is the person that drinks a little of himself with each sip. He, for lack of better words, has become one with the beer or dare I say product.

Ninety-five percent of this book was written in a coffee house. Not any coffee house but one that serves drinks that some say cost you an arm and a leg to buy. At this coffee house you can receive a fancy drink with whipped cream on top. They even have drinks that are made in a blender and some that magically come right out of a giant espresso machine.* But why was I paying $3.00 when across the street they serve (supposedly) the same thing for under a buck? I was going because the coffee was better. It really did taste better and the people were nicer that served it. I was willing to pay more for the entire experience. The trade off was worth it to me at any cost and I'm not alone in this way of thinking. If you have the chance go sit in your local coffee house and count the number of people that come by in any given hour. You'll be surprised and you'll gain great insight on why there is one on every corner.

"Without question, the greatest invention in the history of mankind is beer. Oh, I grant you that the wheel was also a fine invention, but the wheel does not go nearly as well with pizza."

—Dave Berry

With that said, I scream at the top of my lungs, "beer and coffee snobs unite and be proud of your tastes" for we are a small handful of the masses but we know that we are drinking the best stuff around!

What are you doing today to make someone be a snob about you?

**On a side note, most coffee houses' menus are so vast that I would often get a kick out of watching people come in and just stare at the board. Yes, it can be overwhelming but for the sake of all of us behind you please know what you want before the Barista asks you!*

"In Japan, employees occasionally work themselves to death. It's called Karoshi."

—Scott Adams creator of the Dilbert comic strip

SAIM-A-SAY

"Saim-a-say," is what I heard everywhere I went in Tokyo. No matter what store you entered, whether it was a restaurant or clothing store this was how you were greeted. Now take a good hard look at me. Do I look like I can speak Japanese? Why would anyone, let alone someone who is Japanese, think I would have a clue what they were saying?

The answer is because the Japanese care. They are happy that you are in their store. It is not for a love of money but for the mere fact that you are about to share an experience with them. This is your moment and they are here to help with a smile.

Now think about Alcatraz prison. Not the most pleasant thought when thinking of the San Francisco bay but when it's the name of a Japanese hot spot there was no way I wasn't going. Alcatraz, located in the city's hot nightclub area is not so much a tourist trap as it is an excuse for all that is Japanese. These folks know how to let go and create anything they imagine.

Arriving at the restaurant requires that you walk up a long staircase to be greeted by a non-English speaking "jail guard." In fact, no one on the staff speaks English, which only adds to the excitement. Without notice the jail guard handcuffs me to them and leads me to my seat, which really isn't a seat since you take off your shoes and sit on the floor. As I'm being un-cuffed she hands me a menu, which does me no good since it's written in Japanese. I look around and notice two giggling girls seated next to me. Cute like all Japanese girls they speak no English but are more than willing to help. I just point to what they are eating and they understand I want to find it on the menu.

Before my food arrives the two girls and I are chatting away. Well not really but they are showing me their souped up cell phone and I show them my PDA. The communication wall is breaking down, albeit slowly. We even start to exchange photo stickers of ourselves. Half of the time we are laughing and in most cases it is at each other in a friendly way. We end by sharing a dessert together and all is well.

"The only English words I saw in Japan were Sony and Mitsubishi."

—Baseball player Bill Gullickson

We get up at the same time and leave together. We even trade email addresses and promise to stay in touch. As I am about to wave goodbye, they motion that I stay put while they run across the street to the market.

Within minutes they return with a handful of Japanese candy for me. It is a gift for me, which is the customary Japanese thing to do when meeting someone new.

"Color television!
Bah, I won't believe it until I see it in black and white."

—Samuel Goldwyn

I SKIPPED RIGHT OVER IT

TiVo reports that half of its users skip about half of all primetime commercials that air. So how do we as marketers make sure that our commercial falls into the half that get watched?

Easy, we continue to make commercials that not only inform but also engage the viewer. But how are we going to do this? Take this example as your lead, when Interscope/A&M/Geffen Records needed to promote the new albums from label mates Bon Jovi and Counting Crows they chose to take some live footage and tie it in with sponsor Coca Cola and create mini videos that not only spotlighted the artist's work but the soft drink.

Why is the TV Guide channel one of the most popular cable channels to stop and watch after you have picked what you want to watch? Because TV Guide realized that they must give you more than a scrolling list of what's coming on next. They now include regularly scheduled programming. Need to catch the latest movie gossip? They've got it. Music videos? You can even see the latest music videos at thirty past.

TV has been called the ultimate baby sitter and I'm starting to wonder if we should change that to the ultimate adult sitter? How many of us wake up and turn on the TV right away? How many of us flip the tube on right after we drop our workbag on the bed after a hard days work? And who hasn't fallen asleep with the TV on? The opportunities to reach the consumer are there, if only we were paying attention.

Advertisers are betting we soon will be. Can you imagine a pop up ad appearing even as you fast-forward through those commercials? It's coming. And what if that pop up ad allowed you to purchase that item with a simple click of the remote? It's coming.

Don't kill your television just yet.

"I never used to see people walking around listening to music on the streets. Now everywhere I go, I see the iPod's white headphones."

—Moby to Rolling *Stone Magazine*

APPLE IPOD

Enough said.

It will never be the same again.

Ever.*

** Sony's cassette Walkman made its debut in 1979.*

*"Welcome to the Ambush homepage!!!
This page is in support of the rockin'est
band
in the Shreveport (area)."*

—Do these guys rock or what?
http://members.aol.com/billywarn/ambush/

WATCH OUT FOR THE AMBUSH

If you've been in this business for some time, you've probably seen it or been a part of it. Ambushing your competition has become a major force in how companies take advantage of events that they are not necessarily allowed to be at.

Ok, that might be taking it a bit too far but if you are on the receiving end that's how you feel. And if you are on the giving end you usually have a big smile on your face if you've succeeded at your mission.

I have been on the receiving and giving end and while I don't condone the practice I know how tempting it is. I recently had the not so pleasant experience of being ambushed. It was at a concert that took place in a mall's center court. Avril Lavigne was starting the hype machine going for her new record and we had arranged through the record label to be the official radio sponsor of the event. It didn't matter to us that the event was open to the public and any other radio station could say what we were saying without repercussion. That wasn't going to stop us. We owned this event and it was ours.

As you can imagine our competition didn't take too kindly to this and retaliated in the most brilliant way. Even though we managed to shut them out of putting their banners and signage up in the mall, they went on the air saying that anyone spotted with a button they were handing out would win $100 on the spot. The button with its bright colors proudly proclaimed the station's logo and Avril. Before we knew it, they were everywhere. We had been ambushed.

"The Internet is a great way to get on the net."

—Bob Dole

SURF THIS!

When I first entered college the Internet was just green text on a black screen. There were no moving pictures, there was no sound and there certainly weren't any pop-ups! We didn't have MP3s or Instant Messaging either.

What there was were email and newsgroups. My main use for the Internet at the time was trading Grateful Dead bootleg tapes and waiting for an email from anyone that could supply me the set lists from last night's show. Pretty simple, but not much different from what you might use the Internet for now. But we've certainly have come a long way. Below are some sites that receive my attention more often than not nowadays.

www.yque.com: You can bet that the next time a celebrity gets arrested the fine folks at yque will have a "Free 'Insert Celebrity Name Here' T-shirt." Shopping here is great because not only are the T-shirt prices reasonable but you can custom make yours with easy to navigate drop down boxes. Want your Free Michael Jackson T on a blue shirt with red ink? Done. Want your Free Martha or Free Winona T in different colors but both as a tank. Hit yque up now for these and much more including some crazy trucker hats.

www.yes.net: Ever wonder who sings that song you just heard on the radio? Of course you have so now point your browser over to yes.net. Here you can chose the radio station and the time of day and they'll gladly let you know who that song was by.

www.reveries.com: Sign up here to receive a great email each morning with the latest cool news of the day. Tim Manners and his staff do a fine job putting this together each day. I always find something to send on to someone else or just a great idea to file away for a future date.

www.rathergood.com: If you watch VH1 or have ever seen those Quiznos commercials then you are familiar with the singing cats. You know the ones, those lovable creatures that play guitar and scream. Rathergood is where they first got their start and here you can find some classics.

www.camcaught.com: Who cares if MasterCard keeps sending

"During my service in the United States Congress,
I took the initiative in creating the Internet."

—Al Gore in a Wolf Blitzer interview on CNN's *Late Edition* cease and desist orders, I can't get enough of these funny pictures that are a take off on the MasterCard Priceless campaign. Ok, some of them are tasteless and crude but that only adds to them in my opinion. Check out the site and be careful the next time someone is taking your picture or you could end up here.

www.lured.com: Are you in need of a quick idea for a project that just got thrown into your lap? If so, lured.com is the place to go. After a quick sign up procedure, you are free to search the thousands of ideas others have contributed to the website. Highly recommended when those creative juices come to a stop.

www.sethgodin.com: What can you say about Seth Godin except that if you are in this game you better know about him. Godin has written numerous books and ebooks. Sometimes it's hard to keep up with him. And when I find myself in that situation I just take a quick scan of his blog. Godin's one of the reasons for this book.

www.pixeltees.com: This is one of my favorite sites to buy T-shirts from because it not only supports independent artists but the shirts are so fun to make yourself. Check it out and have some fun creating your own pixel art.

xfm.co.uk: This is the online home of XFM radio out of England. When I am in need of getting my fix on the band of the moment in the UK this is where I turn. It is also nice to see and hear what they think of some of our American imports.

"Advertising may be described as the science of arresting the human intelligence long enough to get money from it."

—Unknown

PROMOTE DON'T ADVERTISE

Did you know that eBay didn't start doing mainstream advertising until very recently? At first, the online flea market sent out a press release giving details on how founder Pierre Omidyar started the website to sell his girlfriend's Pez collection.

Starbucks prides itself on how well they treat their employees. Part time employees receive health care benefits along with personal time and their free monthly allotment of coffee beans. And Starbucks isn't afraid to let you know that through the window clings they use to promote the fact that they are hiring and what they bring to the table.

Dean Kamen's Segway story was all told through PR. Before anyone even saw what he was building the hype machine started to roll. The press were told little details about the invention except that it would change the way humans travel. If that didn't get every journalist in the world to start talking and writing about it nothing would.

In the highly competitive world of airline carriers, JetBlue took off (pun intended) roughly a year before an actual plane hit the runway and a few months before they actually had a name chosen. How about that?

eBay, Starbucks, the Segway and JetBlue not such bad company to be in with, huh?

"It is better to die on your feet than to live on your knees!"

—Mexican peasant revolutionary
Emiliano Zapata

PROMOTE DON'T ADVERTISE (PART 2)

Once your company takes off you might get the urge to rest on your laurels but this is definitely not the time to relax. Now more than ever I would implore you to take action. The battle might have been won but the war is still going on in the consumer's minds.

Does Nike still need to advertise on TV and in magazines? Why should they when they are the number one sneaker company in the world? Because they need to continually reach you even though you already have a pair of Nikes in your closet. If they stop, Reebok and the other dozen sneaker makers will gladly take their place in your mind and your closet. Nike knows that being number one didn't happen overnight and they are not going to give up the fight. What Nike sells is more than sneakers. They sell the experience of Nike. If you have ever been in a NikeTown store you know what I mean.* They are brightly lit stores where everything Nike can be obtained. From watches to sport tops to branded MP3 players, NikeTown has it all.

This experience rule can be applied to any category leader. Take eBay who dominates the online auction category, they are currently advertising on TV. Starbucks has billboards all over town promoting their cold drinks and you can't walk into any bar without seeing some sort of merchandise for Budweiser.

Keep at it and never give up!

**Did you know that the famous Nike Swoosh was commissioned for a fee of $35?*

"When in doubt, predict that the present trend will continue."

—Merkin's Maxim

FADS AND TRENDS

There is a huge difference between a fad and a trend and knowing the difference can save you lots of hard work and money. When you know the difference you will also be able to determine where a product is in its life cycle.

A fad will be everywhere you look and you won't be able to escape it. A trend can pass you by and you will be none the wiser. Fads explode while a trend will take its time to emerge itself into the culture. With so much being thrown against the proverbial wall no one can predict a fad but with the right knowledge you can predict a trend. A fad is just the beginning of a trend.

Which is which? Fad or trend?*

A. Reality TV

B. Trucker hats

C. Belly button rings

D. Web blogs

**A) trend, B) fad, C) trend, D) fad*

"Business is not just doing deals; business is having great products doing great engineering, and providing tremendous service to customers. Finally, business is a cobweb of human relationships."

—H. Ross Perot

TURNING BAD INTO GREAT

Every time a special occasion comes around, I have a meal at one restaurant that consistently serves not only the best Kobe steak in town but is known for its customer service. Last night they went above and beyond.

I hadn't been to the restaurant in a few months so you can imagine my surprise when I tried to valet in the usual spot. Turns out they are doing major construction next door and have taken over the parking lot where my car should have gone. We were instructed to park our car a block away where the valet was now set up. Really not such a big deal but it certainly would take away from the expected drive up and walk to the front door in a second routine I had become accustomed to.

Three cheers to the restaurant owner who saw this disadvantage and turned it into what I would call an award winning moment. When I drove up to valet my car I was greeted with the usual fanfare but I was also handed a certificate for one round of drinks on the house for any inconvenience the new parking procedure might have caused. Before I could even begin to get a bad taste in my mouth about the new longer walk to the front door I was put in a good mood courtesy of the restaurant!

The meal as usual was great and the restaurant did itself one up again as I began to leave. At the front door a valet person stood ready to accept my valet ticket. As she did she called out my ticket number into a walkie-talkie so that my car would be waiting as I walked up. There would be no waiting at the end of another fine meal.

"The joy that isn't shared dies young."

—Poet Anne Sexton

SHARE AND SHARE ALIKE

Have you ever wondered why BOGOs (Buy One Get One) offers are so popular? Because they are based on one of the fundamental rules of promotion; sharing between two people.

When your product is good enough to garner buzz your fans will want to share it with friends and there is nothing better than treating someone to something you love. This is a huge motivator for fans and one that they will clamor to be a part of.

If you think you can't afford to be giving away your product, think again. You can turn what might seem like a losing proposition into a winning situation with two simple steps:

1). Reward your fan for bringing someone new into your establishment. Another BOGO or a 10% off coupon will go a long way. Not only will this make your fan appear like a VIP in front of their friend but also it will reinforce in their mind how great a company it is that you run.

2). Be sure to make this new person your next fan. Do your best to make sure that they are taken care of and offer them a BOGO coupon on their way out. If they are treated right, they will gladly bring back a new person to your business and the chain will continue as long as you allow it to.

These two simple rules can easily be done no matter what business you are in. While the above example is great for a retail establishment with a little tweaking it can be applied to any situation.

"If it weren't for Philo T. Farnsworth,
inventor of television,
we'd still be eating frozen radio dinners."

—Johnny Carson

LISTEN AT WORK

Have you ever noticed that radio stations are always pushing you to continue listening even when you get to work? Do you know why? It's because from the hours of 9AM and 5PM there are three rated day parts and that's a lot of missed potential revenue if you're not around.

I was once part of a radio contest that gave listeners the chance to win a jackpot that started at $10,000 and went up from there. The contest was called *What the Hell is That?*, which gave listeners the chance to guess what a secret sound was. If they got it right, they won the amount of money in the jackpot. If they guessed wrong, the jackpot got bigger.

One of the drawbacks for the radio station was that it had a weak signal meaning that it was next to impossible to hear the radio station if you were inside a building. Thus online listening was critical to the station's longevity and ultimately the bottom line. When the listening trends came back in the middle of the contest this fact was clearly shown.

Online listening between 9AM and 5PM was exploding by double digits. Without intentionally setting out to do it, the contest had created a need for listeners to stay informed about the contest and continue listening all day. Would someone get through the ever-busy request lines and give the right answer? Or would the wrong guesses continue to stack up like the pile of money? And even worse would the person that got through guess something that had already been declared the wrong answer, thus wasting a guess?

The need to listen all day lasted as long as the contest did. Once over, online dropped off to a slightly higher number than when the contest started but never reached the astronomical numbers it was doing for a solid three months.

"Don't stay in bed, unless you can make money in bed."

—George Burns

TAKE TIME AND ENJOY YOUR SUCCESS

At the end of the day make sure you take time to enjoy your successes and reflect on your defeats.

I was recently reading *Sleaze* magazine* from the United Kingdom whose cover story was entitled Work Sucks! The one thing that struck me more than anything else in the magazine was the paragraph that told how Americans identify with their occupation first before they speak of what they actually do. Turns out the opposite is true for most of the world. Ask any American what they do and the answer is usually, "I'm an insert job title here." Never is it, "I love to water ski and my wife's specialty is making sushi." Maybe it's time we start thinking differently. Maybe we need to refocus ourselves and come back to the middle and remember why we got in to this gig in the first place.

**Sleaze magazine is available as an import at many finer bookstores across our nation. Each month they directly communicate to the youth of England through words and pictures that speak volumes about what is going on in their country. Many of the pieces can easily translate into what we experience here in the United States.*

"There's a difference between a philosophy and a bumper sticker."

—Charles Schulz

LIVE YOUR LIFE BY A BUMPER STICKER

I've been driving around for weeks staring at the back of cars to try to find some wisdom to take home with me. Here's a sampling of what I found:

A Day Without Sunshine Is Like, You Know, Night
Boy bands. The spawn of Satan.
Cole's Law: Thinly Sliced Cabbage
Do Vegetarians Eat Animal Crackers?
Every silver lining has a cloud.
Forget About World Peace...Visualize Using Your Turn Signal!
Got Brains?
Hang Up And Drive!
I brake for no apparent reason.
Jerry's Dead, Phish Sucks, Get A Job.
Keep honking, I am reloading!
Life May Suck, But It Beats The Alternative.
My Child Beat Up Your Honor Student!
Nobody's Ugly After 2 A.M.!
Out Of My Mind; Back In Five Minutes
Pride Is What We Have. Vanity Is What Others Have.
Quiet Brain! Or I'll Poke You With Another Q-Tip.
Rap Is To Music What Etch-A-Sketch Is To Art
Support Yogurt, It's The Only Culture Some People Have.
Take Me Drunk I'm Home.
Unlike Online, In Reality, You Can't Hit The Back Button.
Vegetarian: Indian Word For Bad Hunter!
We Are The People Our Parents Warned Us About.
You're Not The Boss Of Me!

0-595-32824-5

1803549R0009

Printed in Great Britain
by Amazon.co.uk, Ltd.,
Marston Gate.